Words I Know

A Mouthful of Onomatopoeia

by Bette Blaisdell

Content Consultant:
Terry Flaherty, PhD
Professor of English
Minnesota State University, Mankato

CAPSTONE PRESS
a capstone imprint

A+ Books are published by Capstone Press,
1710 Roe Crest Drive, North Mankato, Minnesota 56003
www.capstonepub.com

Library of Congress Cataloging-in-Publication Data
Blaisdell, Bette.
A mouthful of onomatopoeia / by Bette Blaisdell.
    pages cm.—(A+ books. Words i know.)
Summary: "Full-color photographs and rhyming text introduce and define onomatopoeia"—Provided
by publisher.
ISBN 978-1-4765-3939-3 (library binding)
ISBN 978-1-4765-5099-2 (paperback)
ISBN 978-1-4765-5944-5 (eBook PDF)
1. Onomatopoeia—Juvenile literature. I. Title.
P119.B53 2014
428.1—dc23   2013035689

Editorial Credits
Jill Kalz, editor; Juliette Peters, designer; Svetlana Zhurkin, media researcher; Kathy McColley, production specialist

Photo Credits
Shutterstock: 3445128471, 5 (left), AKaiser, 2–3, 4–5 (back), 32, Alan Bailey, 8 (top), Alexander Cherednichenko, 28
(bottom), altanaka, 8 (bottom), Butterfly Hunter, 20 (middle), cynoclub, 1, Darja Vorontsova, 19, Dmitry Morgan, 17
(left), effe45, 23, Eric Isselee, 5 (right), Erni, 10 (bottom), Ferenc Szelepcsenyi, 18, GGrigorov, 29, haak78, 11, IbajaUsap,
20 (bottom), Illya Vinogradov, 7 (top), InnervisionArt, 10 (top), Irina Tischenko, 28 (top), Jaimie Duplass, 22 (bottom),
Jean Schweitzer, 12 (top), Karen H. Ilagan, 16 (left), Karin Hildebrand Lau, 30 (bottom), kojihirano, 15 (bottom), Marcel
Jancovic, 25 (bottom), Michel Borges, 26, mlorenz, cover, Monkey Business Images, 31, Nanette Grebe, 17 (right),
Natursports, 25 (top), Nomad_Soul, 4 (bottom), oliveromg, 30 (top), PhotoStock10, 24, R. Gino Santa Maria, 14 (left),
Rob Hainer, 9, Samuel Borges Photography, 14 (right), Sandra Caldwell, 15 (top), spotmatik, 12 (bottom), Stephanie
Frey, 22 (top), svic, 20–21 (back), TessarTheTegu, 21 (front), Thomas M. Perkins, 13, Tom Bird, 7 (bottom), Veda J.
Gonzalez, 16 (right), Villion van Niekerk, 6 (top), Volodymyr Burdiak, 6 (bottom), ZouZou, 27

Note to Parents, Teachers, and Librarians
This Words I Know book uses full-color photographs and a nonfiction format to introduce the concept of language and
parts of speech. *A Mouthful of Onomatopoeia* is designed to be read aloud to a pre-reader or to be read independently
by an early reader. Photographs help listeners and early readers understand the text and concepts discussed. The book
encourages further learning by including the following sections: Table of Contents, Read More, and Internet Sites. Early
readers may need assistance using these features.

Table of Contents

What's Onomatopoeia?

Zip goes the jacket.
Grrr says the dog.

That was onomatopoeia
(ah-nuh-mah-tuh-PEE-uh)!

Onomatopoeia refers to words that copy the sounds they are describing.

"Zip" and "grrr" are examples of onomatopoeia. "Zip" sounds like a jacket being zipped up. "Grrr" sounds like a dog's growl.

What kinds of onomatopoeia are hiding inside *your* mouth?

Animal Chatter

What sound do ducks make? Donkeys? Dogs?
How about horses? Hippos? Hogs?

hee-haw

meow

quack

neigh

bark

oink

snort

bray

roar

woof

purr

howl

baa

arf

moo

growl

7

Water Fun

A waterpark is the place to be,
beating the heat and shouting, "WHEE!"

squish
slush
squirt
burble

glug
slap
plop
gurgle

drip
drizzle
swoosh
trickle

splash
spray
splatter
sprinkle

Get Moving

When something moves, listen up!
You might hear "BOING!" or "GLUP! GLUP! GLUP!"

whoosh
click
whizz
tap

clang
flap

clip
zap

plink **snip** clunk **smack**

clank
bang
ring

thwack

Open Wide

This list of words says, "AHHH!" and shows the onomatopoeia in your mouth and nose.

smooch

shh

sniff

wah-wah

grunt

chuckle

yawn

ha-ha

ahem
hee-hee
whistle
hush

snore
yeow
stutter
shush

Two by Two

Sometimes words have more impact
when they star as a double act.

knock-knock

drip-drop

ding-dong

tick-tock

ping-pong
jingle-jangle

pitter-patter

flip-flop

What Did You Say?

So many ways to make yourself heard ...
Read through the list, then pick a word!

bawl
murmur
shriek
grumble

whoop
whine
blab
mumble

giggle

chatter

wail

whisper

snicker

blurt

mutter

whimper

Surprise!

Here's a surprise, just for you.
Will it make you jump or cry, "WHOO HOO"?

bam
clash
boo
gasp

pop
clatter
puff
clap

scream

crack

pow

squeak

thud

tremble

boom

eek

Near the Pond

Critters that hop, crawl, and fly
make noise in the water and the weeds nearby.

hum
buzz
snarl
rustle

rattle
croak
whirr
snap

ribbit drone flitter splat

Catch a Cold

Grab a tissue, and get some rest.
Before too long, you'll be back to your best!

ouch
hiccup
cough
achoo

wheeze
blah
shiver
boo-hoo

sniffle

barf

OW

groan

hack

ooze

gargle

moan

Things That Go

Cars and trucks and things that go ...
Are there words here you don't know?

beep
clink
honk
smash

clack
bump
squeal
crash

rumble
screech
sputter

zoom

rev
shimmy
toot

vroom

Dig In!

Wash your hands. Take a seat.
Grab your fork. It's time to eat!

chomp

rip

slobber

munch

yummy

yuck

gobble

crunch

gulp
gag
slop
burp

spit
belch
fizz
slurp

27

Here, Birdie Birdie

Some sing sweetly. Some sound strange.
Bird calls cover quite a range.

cackle

coo

twitter

peep

caw

tweet

trill

cheep

chirp

cluck

flutter

cuckoo

hoot

squawk

cock-a-doodle-doo

Extra Fun

Onomatopoeia is so much fun!
Want a little more before we're done?

yikes
bumble
crackle
sizzle

bleh
whack
wallop
fizzle

ka-ching
bowwow
clip-clop   choo-choo

poof
kerplunk
zing

yahoo

Read More

Aylesworth, Jim. *Cock-a-Doodle-Do, Creak, Pop-Pop, Moo.*
New York: Holiday House, 2012.

DePalma, Mary Newell. *Bow, Wow Wiggle-Waggle.* Grand Rapids,
Mich.: Eerdmans Books for Young Readers, 2012.

Marsalis, Wynton. *Squeak! Rumble! Whomp! Whomp! Whomp!:
A Sonic Adventure.* Somerville, Mass.: Candlewick, 2012.

Internet Sites

FactHound offers a safe, fun way to find Internet sites
related to this book. All of the sites on FactHound have
been researched by our staff.

Here's all you do:

Visit *www.facthound.com*

Type in this code: 9781476539393

Super-cool stuff! Check out projects, games and lots more at
www.capstonekids.com